LOOKING

FOR

GOD'S COUNTRY

BOOKS BY NORBERT KRAPF

LOOKING
FOR
GOD'S COUNTRY

Poems by

NORBERT KRAPF

TIME BEING BOOKS
POETRY IN SIGHT AND SOUND

An imprint of Time Being Press
St. Louis, Missouri

Time Being Books®
10411 Clayton Road
St. Louis, Missouri 63131

Time Being Books® is an imprint of Time Being Press®, St. Louis, Missouri.

Time Being Press® is a 501(c)(3) not-for-profit corporation.

Time Being Books® volumes are printed on acid-free paper, and binding materials are chosen for strength and durability.

ISBN 1-56809-103-6 (Paperback)

Library of Congress Cataloging-in-Publication Data:

Krapf, Norbert, 1943–
    Looking for God's country : poems / by Norbert Krapf.—1st ed.
       p. cm.
    1-56809-103-6 (pbk. : alk. paper)
  1. Indiana—Poetry. 2. German Americans—Poetry. 3. Franconia
(Germany)—Emigration and immigration—Poetry. I. Title.
    PS3561.R27L66 2005
    811'.54—dc22
                                                            2005001323

Cover photo and section-title photos copyrighted by Andreas Riedel
Cover design, book design, and typesetting by Sheri Vandermolen
Manufactured in the United States of America

First Edition, first printing (2005)

ACKNOWLEDGMENTS

The following poems originally appeared, sometimes in different form and/or with a different title, in these publications: *Blueline* ("Behind Farm Buildings," "Early-Morning Rounds"); *Chariton Review* ("God's Country"); *The Funnel Online* ("Berta and Georg Haberkamm," "Franconian Landscape," "The Ghost Road," "The Man with the Bread," "The Potato Cart," "Shoes Under the Bed"); *The Heartlands Today* ("Patoka River Canoe Trip," "Seining Minnows"); *Heartlands* ("Squirrel Hunter's Dream"); *Ixion* ("Black-Cat Blues," "The Farmer and the Manure," "Going to Church," "Three Saturday Sweepers," "The Village Guards," "The Woman in the Barley," "*Zwetschgenkuchen* / Plum Pastry"); *Long Island Quarterly* ("The Audience of the Dead," "Camp Carnes Facts"); *RogueScholars.com* ("Chicken in the Woods," "Plywood Summer," "The Woman in the Wine Shop," "Women Gathering Apples"); *SpinDrifter* ("The Gardener," "Moon Shadows," "The Nest," "A Pretty Small Town," "Wheel Poem," "Where Trees Are Tall"); *The Texas Review* ("Empty Underground Shelves," "A Fruit Tree After the War, "The Hay-Baler").

"Letter from a Star Above Southern Indiana" was written at the request of the late Governor and Mrs. Frank O'Bannon, of Indiana, for the Hoosier Millennium Celebration and included on the Web site created for that occasion. "Dark and Deep" originally appeared in *Visiting Frost: Poems Inspired by The Life and Work of Robert Frost* (University of Iowa Press, 2005), edited by Sheila Coghill and Thom Tammaro.

The author wishes to thank the editors and publishers of these little magazines, journals, anthologies, and Web sites for giving these poems a previous life. Thanks also to Sheri Vandermolen and Jerry Call, of Time Being Books, for their generous editorial help; John Taylor-Convery, for his helpful response to an earlier version of the manuscript; Helmut Haberkamm, for introducing the author to the work of Andreas Riedel; and Andreas Riedel, for the photographs that inspired the sequence of poems in section two and those which appear on the cover and section-title pages.

For my Franconian brothers:

Helmut Haberkamm, poet, playwright;
Andreas Riedel, photographer

. . . death,
The undiscover'd country, from whose bourn
No traveller returns . . .

— William Shakespeare, *Hamlet*

And whoever walks a furlong without sympathy
walks to his own funeral drest in his shroud.

— Walt Whitman, "Song of Myself"

CONTENTS

III. THE BRANDENBURG GATE

LOOKING

FOR

GOD'S COUNTRY

PROLOGUE

Letter from a Star Above Southern Indiana

It was a crisp fall evening. The leaves were down, smoke was rising from neighborhood chimneys, and I was walking home, across an open field, from a Boy Scout meeting held at the parish school. Usually I keep my eyes on the ground, but on this clear night, as fresh air touched my cheeks, my eyes turned upwards, then soared above our new house at the edge of the woods. What I found in that southern-Indiana sky was "miracle enough to stagger sextillions of infidels," as the great earth-poet Walt Whitman once said. There, burning bright above me, were so many dead stars I could never have begun to count them, if I had wanted to.

What I want to tell you now, wherever you are, whenever you read or hear this, however it is transmitted, is that even though I could not have framed the experience in just these words, even then I knew I was being blessed. Now, a thousand miles and almost fifty years away, I can tell you this: when I made out the shape of the Little Dipper, way above our house, in that little woods in southern Indiana, I felt its collapsed light heading toward me, from thousands and millions of years away. When I also located the shape of the Big Dipper, so high above, I could feel its no-longer-alive radiance pouring down toward the house my parents had built for us children.

At that point, I had not yet seen or stepped inside the brick farmhouse that my father's family had built, with the help of new neighbors, when they arrived from Germany. Framed with tulip poplar from the virgin forest, it stood on a hill just inside the next county. I had not yet discovered that my mother's and father's families once lived about twenty miles apart, in the region of Bavaria known as Lower Franconia. Yet a part of me, the one that is finding these words to beam to you, understood on some level that the family who had crossed the Atlantic on a boat was walking with me, under the stars, toward the house I would later find, so far away, for my wife and children. I could not yet name all those who came before me but felt their presence at my side, knew they were guiding me wherever I would go. I knew I must learn to speak their language, which some of us had already left behind, but which mother and father still spoke.

All who came before were walking with me, toward the new house, as the light poured down on me from millions of light years ago, just as I am walking with you, wherever you are, trying to speak to you in this language I hope is still yours, in this world I hope I still share with you. If you look up, as I looked up, that night in southern Indiana, when the air was so fresh and clear, you may feel the light of this letter falling down toward you. You may even think you can see me in the night sky, will understand that I once walked the earth where you now walk. May this light bless you, your house, and those who come after you.

I.

THE NEST

The Nest

At the edge of the woods
where it comes close to a corner

of the house, between the moist
curves of ferns unfurling in brown

leaves, I found this tiny nest
in the ground. It was lined

with elements that looked to be
soft to the touch. This was right

near Easter. There was squiggly
movement in that lined hole

in the ground. What moved was
newborn rabbits, so tiny you could

barely tell what they were, and I tip-
toed as close as I dared. My mother

told me that if my smell came too close,
the mother would abandon her babies.

I sensed that the difference between
loving and killing was eggshell thin,

but it was hard to control my impulse
to inch closer and closer. Reader,

I cannot be sure if I stayed far enough
away from what I longed to touch

but knew I must not. Is it shame that
blocks me from remembering the out-

come of this backyard tale? Let us join
hands and pray, in our different ways,

that we learn how to control our impulse
to love that which dies if we come too close.

Strawberry-Patch Song

Afternoon sun filled the room
in which I stood, as a boy,

looking out the open window.
My mother was kneeling on stems

of yellow straw, picking red strawberries,
in a blue sundress. As she piled her basket

with layers of ripe berries, the light
coming through that western window

intensified, as if I were climbing
to a higher level of illumination

even though I did not know where
my feet were stepping. I heard her

sing a song that seemed to rise out
of the leafy green plants she was picking,

as much as out of her open mouth:
"I was dancing with my darling

to the 'Tennessee Waltz.'" Whenever
I put a strawberry in my mouth,

break it open with my teeth, and taste
its watery sweetness with my tongue,

I feel the light streaming through
that western window again, see her

kneel between those rows of plants
sagging with berries, and hear her sing

that song as if it came from beyond
her and passed from me to you.

The Gardener

He moved through the garden,
on his afternoon off from selling

insurance, as if it were a preserve
in which he alone controlled

the cycle of birth and death. He knew
well his power and his responsibilities.

His father, though by then long dead,
moved with him at every step,

spoke in his ear when necessary.
He knew just how to sharpen a hoe

with a sandstone he spat onto before
applying it to a dulled edge. He knew

how to turn that hoe at the right angle,
to undercut and remove the weeds

that threatened peas, beans, squash, corn.
He knew how to heap the mounds

of dark earth in which potatoes sprouted
and swelled. He knew what powder to

put on which vegetable, at just the right
point in the growing season, to eliminate

the insects with the appetite to devour.
I can still see him stand there,

in old jeans and straw hat, lift
a red handkerchief from his back

pocket to wipe the sweat off his brow,
limp over to the next row, and begin

to jab that hoe again at the right angle
and swing the big scythe back and forth,

around the edge of the garden, so the tall
weeds fell with a compliant swish.

At the end of the afternoon, my father
would clean and oil every tool, stack

them neatly in the shed he had put up
under the sugar maples, and stand

in the light of the setting sun and savor
the green order he had given the garden.

Chicken in the Woods

Back in the woods near the edge
of our property, Mother carried

a squawking white chicken, by the legs,
in one hand and a hatchet in the other.

She was still a farm girl. She stopped
at a stump, put the chicken's neck

on the flat rings of the amputated tree,
and whacked that chicken's head

clean off, then let go. Blood spurting
all over the leaves, that headless

chicken did a terrible dance of death,
flapped its wings, turned lopsided

circles, until it finally came to rest,
on its side, in the leaves. After those

legs let go, Mother picked up the chicken
and dunked it in scalding hot water.

She plucked the feathers off with deft
fingers, cut the carcass right open,

saved what needed to be saved,
got rid of what could not be used,

and walked back into the house,
ready for her next chore. I saw

splattered blood on those leaves,
even after rain had rinsed it off.

Aunt Justine and the Cistern

A summer guest on the farm
where my mother grew up,
now run by my godfather,
I helped feed the cattle,
bring the cows in from the field,
to be milked, and explored the far
corners of the barn, the smokehouse,
and the woods where my mother
stirred corn mash as a little girl.

When the call came from
the farmhouse, across the fields,
the one in front of which
several generations of Schmitts
posed for a traveling photographer,
everyone jumped into action,
as if they'd done this drill before.

Aunt Justine was threatening
to jump into the cistern again.

Already licensed to drive,
my oldest cousin tore off down
the rock road, in the open Jeep,
and caromed onto the highway,
on two screeching tires.

I stayed behind and wondered
what Aunt Justine could hope
to find in that dark hole where
water stood at the bottom.
What made her want to hurtle
headfirst into that wet darkness?
What must her children,
my cousins, be thinking?
What had the word "cistern"
to do with the concept of "sisters"?

For years, as we drove to the farm
to visit my godfather, I watched
Justine's fence, the house, and the barn
lean into the wind, until they
collapsed, were bulldozed
onto a pile, and burned to ashes
that were plowed into the earth,
where hollyhocks still bloomed.

Justine's dark secrets remain
in that cistern. A round stone
almost nobody sees, in a far field
now farmed by people who do not
carry our name, covers the darkness
festering beneath the surface.

Godfather's Fishing Knife

in memory of Alfred Schmitt

I open the fishing knife
I inherited when he died,
slide my fingertip along the blade,
and flash back to the fishing camp
he shared with buddies, on the bank
of the White River. In the rowboat,
he pulled the trap out of swirling
muddy water, fish flopping
as sunlight flashed on their scales.
He laid out the catfish, perch,
and buffalo on the makeshift wooden
counter nailed to a tree, and the knife
would go to work as if it had a will
of its own. He had no need
to guide it or tell it what to do.
When the guts were all slit and slung
out and the scales scraped clean
and the fillets settled in a bucket
of water, he rolled them in salt
and peppered flour and dropped
them into popping grease until they
turned golden brown. He flipped
them onto a platter next to a plate
stacked with sliced tomatoes from
his garden and coleslaw with enough
vinegar to kill all germs and would
hand me a plate and say, "Here, boy,
eat. You gotta eat to stay alive . . ."

When I close my godfather's knife,
I see him sitting under the sugar
maple beside the farmhouse in which
my mother grew up. He grabs
the handle on the well and ladles
a tin cup of cold spring water
he hands me and then ambles over
to the smokehouse and comes back
with a gallon jug of his Virginia Dare
wine and hands that jug to me and says,
"Here, drink some. A man needs good
homemade wine to stay alive. Never
did make a better batch than this."
As I sip that fruity sweet wine
and smack my lips, I taste how alive
I am when I come into the presence
of this uncle who is my godfather.

Camp Carnes Facts

Up on Eagles' Nest, there was no place
for weaklings, and you were so far

removed from authority you could
do what you damned well pleased;

but the climb up that torturous path
was punishment enough for all your sins.

Down near the mess hall, where all
the sissies and eager beavers slept,

favors and badges could be bought and sold.
Sometimes the food was good, sometimes

it gave you the runs, and once in a while,
in the sandy loam beneath the mess-hall floor,

you could find huge tracks that must have been
left last winter by the Abominable Snowman.

Seining Minnows

Before we dropped our lines
into the big lake, we walked
in the creek, water squishing
in our sneakers, & pulled
a small seine between us.

When we turned & lifted the net,
a mess of minnows flipped back
& forth & caught the sun
on their iridescent sides.

They flipped & flashed
their promise of bigger
things to come, as we spilled
them into a bucket of creek
water & lugged them to the dam,
where we would hook them
through the mouth & dangle
them out over the water,

to settle beneath the surface
& with the flick of a tail
lure something out of the depths
to glide toward a glint of silver
in the murky water & strike
& pull the bobber under & swallow
& yank the line & jerk the pole
almost out of our hands

& tug as if from a heavy dark
world that both thrilled
& frightened us but would
not yield its secrets no
matter how hard we tried
to pull them in.

Patoka River Canoe Trip

We tied the canoes to saplings and crawled
up the bank, to a sandstone ledge, grabbed
the thick wild grapevines, and swung
our feet as far out as possible, before
splashing into the swirling muddy waters
that sucked at our toes and pulled
us downstream. The last one in was
a chicken, and the first one back out
who could slip and slide up the bank
got to fling himself out again, high
over the curent, like a free-flying god
who would never have to come back
to solid earth. Our cries rang out
through the sycamore and cottonwood
leaves and bounced off the trunks.
We were way beyond the grasp
of mothers and fathers and could not
be pulled back any more than the current
could be stopped. Each time we flung
ourselves out over that swirling water,
we left all moorings behind and knew
we would never go home again
and be what we had once been
when we walked out the door.

Patoka River Memories

Near where the old bridge stood
was a mill to which Abe Lincoln
came as a boy. When the bridge
collapsed, we had to detour way
out into the country to get home.
When the Patoka raged one year,
flooding the part of town we called
"Frog Town," we drove through
the waters, slowly, without saying
a single word. Silence was always
the medium in which our parents
negotiated a crisis. One spring day,
I walked home, alone, across the new
bridge, carrying my trombone case
with one hand, thought of my
favorite girl in the class, looked down
at the muddy waters of the swollen Patoka,
and wondered how old and big were
the carp trying to suck the bottom clean.

Early-Morning Rounds

Where rabbit traps stood,
ready to be tripped, I came
every morning, before school,
with a burlap bag slung over
my shoulder. Sometimes I came
home with a wild cottontail
thumping in the bag, sometimes
I came home with an empty bag,
but never did I leave the house
those early winter mornings
without a sense that my bag might
soon come alive with the dark energy
of those creatures of woods and fields.
Every night I crawled in bed full
of anticipation about the excitement
morning would bring as I left home
with a bag slung over my shoulder.

The Hay-Baler

One hot day, a farmer who lived
on the other side of the Patoka River,
on the same land his parents
and grandparents had owned,
did not come in for the midday meal,
from the field where he was baling hay.

His family walked together into the field
and found the baler grinding and groaning
behind an idle tractor sputtering in the sun.

Inside one bale, they saw part
of a mangled arm; in another,
part of a shredded leg . . .

When I read the obit in the newspaper,
I thought of how hungry and neutral
a hay-baler can be, how the wife
and children, the rest of their lives,
would hate the sight and smell
of timothy and clover and lespedeza
and anything green that can be mowed,
raked, dried, and compressed into bales
that can be hauled and stacked in a loft
and thrown for cattle to chew and swallow.

For weeks, I walked with my hunting
dogs to the bank of the Patoka and stared
across the muddy water and brush piles
on the opposite bank, at the field where
that farmer had come to such a violent end,
on a spot of earth he knew and loved.

I wondered how his children could
bear to set foot again on the ground
of that field where they had suffered
such a loss that my imagination
could not begin to comprehend
what they must feel and think.

Barnyard Hoops

We shot hoops at night,
in the barnyard, off a backboard
nailed to the side of the barn.
There was a light that poured
rays on us like misty rain.
At first the coonhounds barked
when we began to dribble
on the hard-packed earth,
but they gave up and fell asleep
when we found our touch.
You couldn't always see if
the ball went in, but you could
tell by the sound of the swish.
A gallon of homemade wine,
swiped from someone's cellar,
was stashed off to the side
as a pickup for any sagging spirits.
When the full moon came out,
you could shoot the eyes out
of the basket, but you could
not find that hoop, today, in broad
daylight. A shopping mall and a big
black parking lot stand where,
once upon a time, in the night air,
you could hear that leather swish
inside a cord net like the sound
of an angel landing in heaven.

After the Football Game

Gary was driving Dimp home,
in his stick shift, after the game
we had won. When they approached
Dimp's house, the car ahead of them
was going too slow, so Gary dropped
it into second, stomped it to the floor,
pulled out to pass, and crashed head-on
into a car coming the other way.

When they pulled Dimp out
of the car, he was no longer breathing.
They laid him on the front lawn,
not far from the mailbox on the post.

When Dimp's parents woke up
that night, to the sound of that
concussion, what they thought
is beyond my ability to grasp,

except when I sit up, in bed,
with the reading light on,
waiting for my teenage son to bring
the car back home, he turns
into the driveway, and I hear
the sweet crunch of tires on rocks,
take a deep breath, turn off
the light, and try to fall asleep.

Urban the Caretaker

A bachelor who worked
for the Park Board as if
he were a convict turned cop,
Urb patrolled his beat –
two parks, two tennis courts,
and two baseball fields –
in a battered red Chevy pickup
he hurtled like a torpedo
from one crime scene to another.

He had a hawk's eye for rotten
carrion, hit the brakes as if he
were pounding your stomach,
and jumped off the running board,
ready to spear hot-dog wrappers,
crumpled paper cups, dried-up
rubbers, on the run. "Kids, goddamn
kids!" he mumbled. "They sure
ain't what they used to be!
All they do is make a mess."
His brothers' kids were by far
the worst, had ten times more
toys than he ever did on the farm,
where he'd had to make his own.

Urb laid down the straightest line
of lime from home to third you
ever saw, knew how to sharpen
a power-mower blade so you
could use it to shave the shadow
right off your chin, could start,
in an instant, any engine that
didn't want to turn over,
by giving it a mean look.
He could spot an empty beer bottle
from a block away, knew how
to gather and save bottles and turn
them in at the end of the summer,
to throw a party for him and his helper.

After two beers, Urb mellowed,
asked if you knew he'd gone
to barn dances with your dad,
"who scraped a mean fiddle."
"No? Well, I could tell you stories
would singe the hair off your
you-know-what. You kids think
you invented good times, don't you?
Kids, goddam kids. Always the same!"

Plywood Summer

In the muggy Indiana summer, a crew
fed strips of veneer through glue rollers,

layered them between sheets of metal,
on the table we wheeled toward the press,

fed them into different levels, pulled
the switch, and watched those jaws

clamp shut like a series of angry vices.
Temperature in that sweaty concrete-

block inferno rose to beyond bearable,
as the press sizzled and cooked that

veneer into plywood. When the load
was done, we opened the press, and glue

steam puffed out and stung our eyes
and nostrils. Chief, my buddy from

the southeastern neck of the county,
with the ruddy face and high cheekbones,

always carried the impression of a half-
pint bottle in the back pocket of his

overalls. Many mornings he never
made it to work. As soon as the whistle

blew at the end of the day, I lit and puffed
a Lucky Strike, ached to smack the cover

off a softball, and longed to tap that pony
of beer as soon as the league game was over.

Wheel Poem

You won't believe this, but the phone
company paid me to walk and measure

the distance between poles in the country.
Yes, that's right, one of us pushed this

wheel between poles, and the other
kept the charts on distances between,

numbers of lines and brackets on poles,
and any equipment oddities. Lots of time

to appreciate trees and woods, examine
wildflowers on the side of the rock road,

listen to the various songs of birds,
and wonder how far away the car was.

For noon break, backed the car into woods
and had frontseat and backseat snoozes.

No boss could ever find where you were!
If you had a partner like Charlie,

who had a car and didn't like to talk,
you had pasture enough for your imagination

and room enough for some big-time fantasies.
Only you could decide whether to share them.

The Storyteller

Once there was a man
who loved to tell stories,
not about himself but about
other people, those who did
not believe their lives could
become the stuff of stories
anyone would want to hear.
He had the eyes and ears
to find stories everywhere
he looked and listened. His
mission was to give shape to
and share what he saw in others
and pass on their stories to
anyone who would lend an ear.
This man had a voice that
was gentle but strong enough
to make you stop what you
were doing and follow where
his voice led. As the man
who loved to tell a tale grew
older, his voice deepened
and more and more people
followed him around, to hear
what came out of his mouth.
When he died, they had
him cut open, to find out
what made him such a great
storyteller. All they learned
was that he had a heart like
a hammer, lungs like a bellows,
and traces of a spirit their
probing fingers could not
quite touch or define. Soon
after they laid his body
in the earth, his stories
came to life in every home
and on every street and were
passed down by father to son,
mother to daughter. The man
*

who loved to tell stories came
back to life in these stories
that people loved to tell,
because now they were about him
but had become part of them.

The *Schneebrunzer*

There was a boy you may
have known who came
into his own when it snowed.
His art was so private no one
saw him practice it, but he left
his artifacts for all to enjoy,
so long as they did not melt.
You might turn a corner
downtown and find a yellow
I in the gutter. Behind
a tree in the park would
be burned a big *U*.
Sometimes when ambition
filled him like a balloon,
he would etch the outline
of a yellow rabbit against
sparkling white or wriggle
a snake that disappeared
into a steaming manhole cover.
They say that, once, after he
got into his father's cache
of beer in the refrigerator,
he left his signature
on the sidewalk behind
the church: *The* Schneebrunzer
lives! Mothers and fathers
would point, children would
giggle, and the mayor offered
a reward to anyone who would
reveal his identity; but the *Schnee-
brunzer* kept his name and his
art to himself. He came to
understand that his tenure
as artist, on this earth, was finite
and that all things must pass.

II.

FRANCONIAN
FACES AND FIELDS

What the Map Says

When we look at a map
of routes that brought them
from the Old World to the New,
we cannot help but come
with them wherever they go.

We bring with them
the expectation of finding
something they did not
have where they had been.

We shake in fear
of losing what they
had to leave behind
in the shape of those
waving long goodbyes.

We sigh in relief
at no longer having
to contend with what
had become unendurable.

Every line we follow
is a series of steps
we take in the direction
of a new life we believe
is coming toward us.
We call that hope.

Every line we look back on
is a wake of water fanning
wider and wider behind us,
until it subsides and disappears.

Where we are sailing
is who and what we
become and the legacy
we build as we move
toward a future we make
for those who follow.
We call this love.

The names we find
on the passenger lists
have a half-familiar ring:
those we once were,
those we have become.

That language we hear
them speak in the hold
is the tongue we once spoke
or an inflection in the speech
we had to learn when we
touched on a new shore,
took a new kind of step.

When we look at this map,
all the lines and routes
lead in the directions
of where we once came from
and where we have gone.

We call this history,
we read it with eyes
that see both ways at once,
and we bring it with us
wherever our steps take us.

We hang this map
of our history on the wall,
for those who come
after, and we put our
fingertips on all the dots
that connect and show
what leads to ourselves.

Franconian Faces and Fields:
After Andreas Riedel

1. Road

It stretches straight ahead.
You cannot see where it ends.
There are no houses
or farm buildings
and no people
and no animals,

but there are leaves
scattered here and there
and trees stripped bare
and fields on either side.

There are no cars
and no trucks,
no tractors,
no motorcycles.

All you hear
is the hush
of the place.

What you feel
is the people
who have walked
down this road,
for many generations

and the clopping
of the hooves
of horses
and the rolling
of wagon wheels

and the neighing
of a horse

and the whisper
of wind that
blows at dusk

and the patter
of rain that falls.

2. Franconian Landscape

In the foreground,
dark tilled soil
so rich you
want to taste it.

Beyond that,
rows of what is
now nothing but
a trace of stubble.

Then a hedgerow
of saplings and bushes
that drops off
to a valley below.

On this level,
trees and a white
road running
at an angle
to a destination
cut off from view.

Land rising
to the right,

and to the left
a village with
a church spire
whose tip is
barely visible

and the hint
of mountains
way beyond,

to which one
day the spirits
of the people
of this place
shall return.

3. The Ghost Road

You stand and look out
over a field of wheat
that ripples and rolls
farther than you can see.

When you recover
from the dazzle of sunlight
playing on golden brown,

you see two parallel
lines or traces
of an old ghost road

looping and bending
toward the horizon
and infinity beyond.

What spirits hover here,
waiting for harvest?
Whose breath blows
over this grain?
Whose voices whisper
when breezes blow?

4. The Curve of Farm Buildings

Sometimes when you
see old farm buildings,
you feel things
you forgot were
part of you before
you moved away.

The way buildings
stand and slope
together, in a line
that forms a curve,
brings you inside.

Now you are back
to when you heard
the splash of milk
in a bucket, in a rhythm
that was a Morse code

and you heard
the splatter of urine
and the plop of dung

and you were
warmed by the breath
of animals standing
by your side

and you loved
to roll on bales
of straw in the loft....

When you find
yourself back outside,
looking at the curve
of old farm buildings,

you realize they
must be much like
the ones in which
those who gave
you your name
once lived.

5. The Farmer and the Manure

He stands in the Hof,
with his back against
a wagon full of manure
from stalls he has cleaned
with his pitchfork.

The earthy grin that's
close to a smile tells
you he would much rather
carry the sweet scent of animal
shit in his wide-open nostrils,
through his daily chores,

than inhale the poisons
of the city or the stale
air of the suburbs.

He would much rather kill,
with his hands, the meat
that he eats rather than buy
a Styrofoam package, wrapped
in plastic, in the supermarket.

Though his grin resembling
a smile reveals teeth worn
down to nubs, spaces
widening between them,

barrel-chested Adolf Müller,
rumpled hat on his head,
says, in no uncertain
but unvoiced words,

that he stands squarely
in the middle of his
family's *Bauernhof*,
on stained cobblestones
he will not hose clean,

and there is no way
he will ever budge
from this place he has
known and loved for
as long as he has lived.

6. Berta and Georg Haberkamm

She stands in her kitchen,
leaning on a counter,
looking straight at you.
Nothing is concealed;
all is revealed.

Her hands are folded
together as if to say
to work is to pray.

The slight smile,
blessed by sunlight,
speaks acceptance
of what she was given
to do with her life.

She moves slowly
about her domain,
the kitchen of this
Franconian farmhouse,
does not take
one false step.

Her husband, Georg, stands
not very far away.
They move together,
as if they had learned
to walk on the same floor.
All four feet are
always on the ground.

Always they think
and talk about their
children and grandchildren.

Where they live
is what they love.

7. Hans and Marie

They stand in front
of the door
of a wooden shed,
caught between chores,
and smile as if to say:

*Why are you
interested in us?
We are doing
what we have done
every day of our lives,
just what our parents
did every day
of their lives,
what our grandparents
did before them.*

Hans' head
is covered
with a cap,
Marie's with
a textured scarf.

She holds work
gloves in her hands.

He wears an apron
held up with twine,
she several layers
of bright patterns.

Look: his right hand
touches her left.

They love not
only their work.

8. Suspenders

When a man
stands straight
and puts his hands
around the bottom
of the suspenders
that hold up his pants
and leaves the top
button of his plaid
shirt open, so his chest
hair curls and glistens,
and sunlight gathers
on the tip of his nose
and his lips form
a smile, you know
he will stride right
into the middle
of another day
and give himself
to the work at hand.

9. Julius at the Door

Julius Schmeisser stands
sideways against a double
door with long hinges. One
hand is cocked on his hip;
the other arm leans against
the grains of the wood.
As soon as you look away,
Hans will swing these double
doors wide open and step back
into the work he has always
done and always shall do.
Hans is lean and wiry
and tough and would never
have it any other way.
His rugged work shoes
stand on stone that has lasted
a long time, and every step
he takes will lead him
in the direction in which
he has always been going.

10. Behind Farm Buildings

Behind farm buildings,
where people rarely come,
stand long stacks of wood
in winter mist and fog.

Beneath bare trees,
behind farm buildings
where the eye does not
usually come, cut and split
wood, its grain exposed,
is stacked, crisscrossed,
in rows that run as far
as the eye can see
whenever it does come
to rest on a scene like this.

Nobody stands here,
behind these farm buildings,
where firewood stands
stacked with such care
and ready for use,

but someone must have
worked a long time
to cut, split, and stack
so much good wood,
with so much care.

Someone must come
to carry away a load
of this wood to place
in the stove and warm
the rooms where people
sit and eat and talk and sleep
and laugh and cough and cry,

but who came or comes
here to tend to this wood
is not part of what the eye
can perceive when it comes
to rest behind farm buildings.

11. Shorn Sheep

Shorn sheep, seen
from above, walking
away from the shears,
across a black floor:

snow-white fetuses
floating in a dark sea,

tufts of wool bobbing
in amniotic fluid, as far
as the eye can see.

12. Anna's Oven

Through the open
door of Anna's oven,
you can see loaves
that have risen
and will absorb
the heat of the fire
and turn dark brown
and have such texture
and pack such flavor

that when you cut one
slice and take a bite
and feel it settle
in your stomach,

you know you were
born into the right
world and have found
the right food to keep
you breathing there.

13. The Man with the Bread

When a man walks
down the Hauptstrasse
with a basket full
of fresh bread, people
feel his mysterious power
and get out of his way,

for the shapes of doughy
freshness he carries
with a sense of mission
give off rays of energy
everyone feels and needs.

He might look ordinary,
and he might look old,
but what he carries
in his wicker basket
keeps people alive,
makes them feel
the beat of their heart
when the fresh bread
touches their tongues.

This wafer of life,
this miracle of grain,
ground and mashed
to a powder and mixed
with milk, egg, yeast,
and a touch of salt,
finds its own level
when transformed in fire

and comes out in shapes
people love to touch and hold
and cut and slice and butter
and glaze with jellies
and jams, or layer
with cheeses and meats.

When you see the man
toting this miracle
in a basket come walking
down the Hauptstrasse
early in the morning,
you know the waters
will part, the traffic
will stop, the noise
will die, and the multitudes
will certainly assemble,

for the man with the bread
has come through the desert,
crossed over the mountain,
and found his way back
to our ordinary town.

He's bringing the food
we have not tasted fresh
for twenty-four hours,
he's walking our streets,
looks like one of us,

and we stop whatever
we're doing and put
our feet under his table,

for the man with the bread
has come home again.

14. The Woman in the Barley

She rises up
out of ripe barley,

one hand holding
several tassels
of grain,

the other grasping
a cycle she's
poised to swing.

As the barley
turns golden brown
before your eyes,

gray hair turns blonde,
wrinkles vanish,
smile widens, lips
part slightly, one eye
opens and beckons,
her clothes fall
off like chaff,

and we see
the goddess
of grain stand
ripe in the sun.

15. *Zwetschgenkuchen* / Plum Pastry

To see these split plums
flipped onto their backs,
on top of sweet dough,
like victims to be
offered to the gods,

is to think of
what hangs beneath
a man's member

or the cloven line
at the center
of a woman.

Take a piece
in your hand,
lift it to your mouth,
take a good bite,

and you will
be lifted up
by the combination
of sweet and tart

that hits you
like the bite
of a good lover.

16. Eva's Knife

Eva stands strong,
in her apron
at the block table,
holding a razor-
sharp knife.

All her life
she has been
ready to cut.

In front of her
lies a slab of pork
begging to be
sliced into bacon.

The veins standing
out in her hand
holding the knife
ready to cut
match the furrows
of intensity
lining her forehead.

Eva's mouth is pursed
for the cut, but she's
caught in midaction.

Flash ahead: bacon
sizzles in a pan,
reheated drippings
turn sliced onions
transparent, boiled
potatoes cooled in
their jackets and sliced
thin absorb flavors
of bacon and onion.

From the cut
of Eva's knife
comes this alchemy
of the kitchen.

17. Women Gathering Apples

They have driven a tractor
pulling a wagon to this spot
that has drawn them here before
and parked it in the shade
and filled wooden crates stacked
on the wagon. They are under
a tree that fans wide and full,
windfall is scattered on the ground,
sun shines on the field beyond,
and they bend over to gather
the best, to put in wicker baskets.
They have done this slow dance
of touching the ground, before,
and they will do it again,
until they can no longer breathe
and are laid, in wood, into this earth.

18. Apples in Rainwater

In a puddle
of rainwater
that collected
between a growth
of weeds, beneath
an old apple tree,

these full globes
fell and rolled
together in just
the right way,

to find morning
sunshine that makes
them look like
orbs of gold,
compact bursts
of luminosity,

gifts brought
and left here
by the three
wise men,

as they passed
on their way
from the East.

19. Three Saturday Sweepers

Every Saturday afternoon
they emerge from somewhere,
these sisters of darkness,
to sweep the street clean
for Saturday night
and Sunday morning.

Maybe they are a Franconian
version of Shakespeare's
weird sisters from *Macbeth*,

but what they know
how to do is
clear all the dreck
left by others
off the Hauptstrasse.

They have been
doing their Saturday dance
of keeping it clean
with the bristles
of their brooms
for so many centuries

you would not dare
get in their way
or tell them to stop.

The road through
the center of the village
must be kept as clean
as the top of their stoves.

If you dare step
into their way,
not only will your shoes
come away caked
with something that stinks,

but you may lose
the power to love
and purchase a place
in the world to come.

20. Woman with a Rake

When this farm woman
in long dark dress
covered with white curlicues
and polka-dotted shawl
tied under her chin
pulls a long-handled rake
through hay her husband cut,

her mother and grandmother
pull with her on the handle,
and she feels the strength
of generations beyond.

She knows that to work
is to live, and to live fully
is to feel that you stand
in a long line with those
who came before
and those yet to come.

21. Women in Potato Field

When potatoes swell
like the stomach
of a woman with child,

reach the maximum
of their potential,
and lie in rows
between mounds,

who has time to stand up
and look at who's coming
across the field to talk?

To touch and possess
these potent tubers
is to feel the power
of water boiling on the stove
that renders the hot starch
soft for the fork,
delectable for the palate,
warm in the stomach.

Who could stop filling
woven wicker baskets
with their roundness

and trudge back
to the farmhouse
with the weight
of these fleshy stones

balanced in baskets
that keep you tied
to the earth,

with the promise
of nourishment
to sustain a family,
if not a clan,
through the cycles,
seasons, and tribulations
of one more year?

22. The Potato Cart

Someone is rich.
Someone has buckets
and baskets of potatoes
stacked on a cart.

Someone is ready to go
and will surely go far.

If you have an ample
supply of potatoes,
you can go anywhere,
and children and lovers
will follow you
wherever you go.

Potatoes are gas
in the tank,
money in the account,
ink in your pen,
indulgences for the soul,
light in the dark.

If you know what you
are doing, potatoes can
even give you vodka
to sip as you go,

not just meat
and gravy heaped over
mounds and boulders
of white pleasure,
at the side of the road,

not just dollops
of mashed whiteness
holding a pond of dark
gravy, in the middle
of the country.

Who has potatoes
has the means
to go anywhere
at any time,
can barter and trade
with people all
over the world.

It all comes down
to one principle:

who has potatoes
shall inherit the earth!

23. The Village Guards

Two women stand in a drizzle,
backs against a house. One,
her mouth pressed shut like
a vice, holds an umbrella
bordered with flowers. The other,
her mouth wide open as a hungry
baby bird, stands in the moisture,
a scarf tied over her head.

They both stare at the same sad
development, whatever it may be,
but only the one holding an umbrella
hears what her good friend says.

Someone may have run a red light.
Someone may have dropped a scrap
of paper on the street. Someone may
be wearing a skirt that's too short
and walking in the wrong kind of way.
Someone may have shouted a word
never to be heard in this kind of town.

Whoever the culprit, whatever
the crime, the women will stand
in the drizzle, one with her mouth
closed, one with her mouth wide open,
and nothing will change, and nobody
will stop, and by midnight the drizzle
will have licked the filthy street clean.

24. Black-Cat Blues

The *Gasthaus* is still closed,
the beer taps have dripped dry,
the stove is cold in the kitchen,
and the *Stammtisch* is as quiet
as the church on Saturday night,

when out on the sidewalk,
at the first crack of dawn,
struts the meanest-lookin' black
cat these poor eyes ever did see.

Lord, have mercy, I'll never
drink one too many again;
I'll go to church every Sunday
and every First Friday too,

if only you make that mean
ol' black cat keep struttin'
his stuff down the Hauptstrasse,
right past the *Gasthaus* front door.

25. Going to Church

All dressed up
in their Sunday best,
white shirts, suits, and ties,

one holds his hat
in his hand, next
to his prayer book;
the other wears
it on his head.

They both smile.
They are moving ahead
as if entering the curve
on the last lap of a race
at a very good pace.

They are dressed to the nines.
No way could they look any better;
two old men going to church.

The way they smile,
the way they move
with such grace,

says ladies they love
are going to church, too.

26. Shoes Under the Bed

What story can two shoes
left under a bed tell?

Someone has come a long way
to find the right place
to lay down a weary head?

Someone will be ready
to spring out of bed
and begin morning chores?

Someone who has never
left here can't wait
to walk away and explore
a world he's never seen?

Someone is lonely and waits
for another pair to arrive?

Someone has died,
and those he loved
don't know what to do
with these vessels that
carried him to his last rest?

One thing seems certain:
these shoes were made
for coming back home.

III.

THE

BRANDENBURG GATE

The Brandenburg Gate: Berlin, 2000

I am sitting on a bench in the middle of Unter den Linden, with the lindens in luxuriant and sensual bloom, on a beautiful but hot sunny day. I walked from the Wiener Café, near Charlottenstrasse, all the way to the Brandenburg Gate. I wanted to stand and look at the famous symbolic arch from the East, looking West, just as in 1981 and 1989, I stood looking from the West toward the East. Now I am here, in what was the East, to read my poems in a world that was closed off to me, unless I came as a tourist on a bus, not as a poet to share his words and vision of life, with young people. It feels good to enter a world that once seemed beyond the reach of my life, my generation, and my children, who know how to speak the language of this country.

I say open the gates, let people walk toward one another. Let us learn how to walk with one another, with those who came before, with those who will follow after. Let poems and songs help break down the walls separating our places and our people! Let language, the right language, the language of heart, mind, and soul walking in balance . . . let this language that comes from deep within a people and their history . . . let this language bring us in touch with one another and all we may share. Let this pure language flow.

Empty Underground Shelves

Humboldt University, Berlin

I stand on the spot where the Nazis
burned books at this university in 1933,
look through a Plexiglas window

in the cobblestones, and stare
at a hollow underground room,
where walls of empty shelves stand.

The longer I look, the more I hear
the silence of those whose pages
fed that fire and whose words

were released into the elements to climb,
like small stars, into the sky and look
back down and shine like sparks

when we gaze into the night sky.
The voices of those who were burned
begin to moan, then murmur

like a sad choir that has not yet
found its collective voice, but the longer
I listen, the more I hear the murmur

approach the right resonance. I stand
in the presence of those who were burned,
and they rise in me as I walk

away with a hum in my ears and
a hurt in my heart. An animal howl
escapes from the hollow room

I carry away with me, and I leave part
of myself squatting, in silence, on empty
shelves, where pages of books should be.

Würzburg Sequence: After Gunter Ullrich

1. Riders over Würzburg

Over the city,
from whose buildings
flames leap and lick
like tortured tongues,
writhing ghosts,
twisted tulips,

and around church towers
and howling hollow
facades, structures
reduced to walls
and windows through
which nothing but
Hades-hot air
sucks and hisses,

ride Dürer's Four
Horsemen of the Apocalypse,
horses' hooves raised
in midsky, swords,
bows, and truncheons
held ready on high,

as tails give off
tracers of flame
and bee-black bombers
drone in formation
below, soar west,
and disappear
into the darkness.

2. Black Sun, 1945

The sun hangs
charred black
the morning after
the bombs exploded,
its brightness
burned to a crisp.

The twin towers
of the cathedral
glow a ghostly
white mixed
with ashen gray.

A dark hole gapes
between towers
where colored glass
once caught light.

In a courtyard,
in the shadows
of the towers,
lie the crumbled bones
of Walther von der
Vogelweide, singer
of songs gone silent.

A pink glow
flickers on facades
left standing,

hellfire this
dead city's only
illumination.

Down the dead street,
where no souls walk,
lies the Old Main
Bridge, back broken,
artery severed,
collapsed, in fragments,
into the black waters
oozing over the heads
of the stone statues
of the saints lying
on their backs
on the bottom
of the river.

3. Destroyed Facade

St. Peter's Church, Würzburg, 1945

How could
the percussion
of firebombs
dare crack this
holy facade,

sending fissures
through stone
that had stood
for centuries,

leaving portals
and arches
open to
the elements,

flames guttering
where candles
had flickered,

columns and
capitals collapsed
onto a heap,

onto which rain
falls as rat
tails rustle?

4. A Fruit Tree After the War

When he rode the tank
into his hometown,
the firebombed Würzburg,
the baroque buildings
were collapsed.

Little was left standing
against a dark sky
except silhouette walls
with windows opening
into nothingness
within and beyond.

Rubble, rubble
of blasted stone
and burnt wood
made the odor
of ash lodge
in the nostril.

Gray, gray
mixed with black
as far as the eye
could see, and ghostly
traces of red.

The only sound
was the lowly lick
of fire still finding
refuse to consume.

Something lifted
his depressed eye
to a palette
of color against
this backdrop:

on charred branches
of a fruit tree,
maybe peach,
maybe cherry,
sometimes white,
sometimes pink,

fluttered pale,
fragile blossoms
all the more
luminous

for the gray
and ash against
which they hung.

5. What Survives

for Gunter Ullrich

There are no people
in the pictures
or in the poems
about the pictures,

but who dropped
the bombs from the sky,
onto the buildings?

Who was inside the buildings
when the bombs fell
and exploded into flame
that raged down the streets
and into those buildings?

Whose flesh burned
when the flames flared
and licked and spread
and buildings collapsed
in that awful night?

Who later drew,
then etched, the destroyed
facades of the buildings
and saw the Four Horsemen
in the dark sky
over the burning city
and put a blackened sun
in that infernal sky?

Who wrote the poems
about the dead city
and loved the blossoming
fruit tree in the etching
of the city in ruins?

Who says there are
no people in the buildings
and no people in the poems
about these buildings

also says that what
survived the death
and destruction
in the buildings
and in the poems
is what lives on
within people,

is indeed not only
the spirit of the people
in the buildings
or in the poems

but the spirit which
survived in the people
then and still lives
now and forever, here
and elsewhere, amen.

A Quiet Corner in Thuringia

for Helmbrecht Breinig

Here in the woods
climbing above the valley,
Solomon's seal, lily
of the valley, and ivy
run with summer rain
that falls from leaves
high above our heads,

as we come to pay
our respects at the graves
of the parents and grandparents
of my friend who lives
in Franconia, to the south.

His mother and family
left here in the 1920s,
never to come back,
until he could arrange
to have his parents' ashes
sent to the authorities,
in 1976, brought home,
and made part of this
peaceful piece of earth,

which he had to reclaim
as private property,
after reunification,
just beyond the end
of the village cemetery
the officials plan to lock,
and he must secure a key
for the local couple
who serve to give
this spot the right care
and the touch of flowers.

As we stand still
in this quiet corner
of the world, rain
drips on our foreheads,
the heart returns to its
origins, and the dead
wait for and receive us
with a patience beyond
our power to know.

The Woman in the Wine Shop

She receives my friend and me
with a gentleness that puts us
at our ease, appreciates that he
wants a good but not too expensive
bottle of wine for an important
occasion, the birthday of a friend.

Her light brown hair, which
she could let flow, is tied back.
She is dressed in soft denim.
Her pale blue eyes ripple
with a warmth that burns
like a low flame she will
not allow to flare higher.

She gives us a graceful but
understated tour of all her
shop can offer, says what
is appropriate, but no more,
for each bottle of wine that
might suit such an occasion.

With a smile that does not say
too much, she lets my friend
come to his own conclusion.
When he selects just the right
wine, she nods and smiles again,
as if to confirm his good taste.

Although her eyes do not open
in the wrong kind of way,
it is hard not to let yours
come to rest on hers,
so delicate and warm.

You can tell she understands.
What is not said often says
more than what is said.

Some eyes are for looking,
some are for looking into,
some may be for touching,
but there are also blue eyes
that know they should remain
open enough for others
to enter but not so far they
can wander where they
know they should not go.

Petra in Her Garden

I look up from my desk,
where I write in my journal,
and see Petra, all in black,
bend over to pour rainwater
from a green sprinkling can
onto a hydrangea bush
loaded with buds.

Her build is trim, her
features finely chiseled,
her brown hair short,
her eyes pale blue,
but she is still
a Franconian farm girl.

As she bends over
to water this bush
laden with flowers to be,
her mother and grandmother
stand on either side of her
on the family farm.

The weight of her father's
illness presses on her
slight shoulders and back.

As Petra, a nurse, pours
life-giving water in her
garden in the suburbs,
she dreams of a farmhouse
out in the country.

Green grows on every side
of her house. A garden stretches
with rows of vegetables. Pink
and blue flowers bloom in beds.
A toolshed is filled with
all that she needs to tend
what she grows. A rooster
crows; hens cluck in a coop.

Between her country house
and garden stands a gazebo,
the trellises of which
are twined with lush vines
and heavenly blue morning
glories cupping the dew.
This is where Petra repairs.

Schroeder the Franconian Cat

As the American guest writes at his desk,
in an upstairs bedroom, he looks down
at the sunlit garden and sees Schroeder,
a Franconian cat named after an American cartoon
character, repining on a wooden chaise longue.
As his mistress pours rainwater on a hydrangea
bush in the corner, Schroeder twitches his ears
at the cooing of turtledoves, turns his back
on the songless starling nesting in a bird box
nailed to an evergreen along the fence.
"Flowers, to hell with flowers," he growls.
"Bring me my Sunday cartoons from the land
of catfish and caviar! The service
is terrible here! Maybe I should move
to a richer corner of the Reich." *And where,
oh where, is my master,* he wonders, *in his
study, scratching out more dialect poems?
Give me a break!* He rolls over on his side,
curls up in a ball, dreams of a carp from a local
pond, a trout from high in the Schwarzwald,
a herring from the North Sea, by Bremerhaven.
"My kingdom for just one fish!" he meows.

The Girl in the Garden

after a sculpture by Ursula Ullrich-Jacobi

Elbow on her knee,
head on her hand,
she sits staring
down and away.

Part of her long hair
falls onto a breast,
part down her back.

One arm, bending across
a leg tucked up against
an inner thigh, covers
the divide at her center.
Full lips press together.

To have fallen into darkness,
to be lost in thought about
what you may or may not
become, to be looking for
what cannot yet become
visible or a shape not
yet ready to emerge into
your life, is to be removed
from what makes you
beautiful in the eyes
of those who see you
from the outside only.

So there is nothing to say
to her as last light of day
falls on the side of her hair,
making her glow blonde.

All you can do is place
a hand on the back
of her neck and hope
she feels it there when
she returns from where
she has gone, to what makes
her so beautiful to you,
where you stand at her side.

Spark and Flame

Uta stands tall in the sunshine,
bends to look through an open door
of a nineteenth-century blacksmith's shop.
She raises her right hand, almost
as if in blessing, to point out how
her father once worked in such a forge,
making horseshoes and wagon wheels.

There is such tenderness
in her voice, such warm light
in her pale blue eyes,
such gentleness in the curve
of her outstretched hand
as she explains how her
father shaped hard iron
into usable shape, in the fire,

that I see her sitting by his side,
in the shadows, as a little girl
watching sparks rise as he
pounds and shapes glowing
iron against the anvil.

She is the young muse
who fans the flame
of his creation.

When I look back
from the fire I think
I see still burning inside
the old forge, I notice
streaks and patches of red,
in her brown hair, that spark
and flame as sunshine
lights the soft lines
of her face and lips.

The Blacksmith's Daughter

When she sees
a metal sculpture
of a beautiful girl,
her father's blacksmith fire
burns in her imagination.

She remembers iron
as a material
only heat and power
can master.

As a girl, she watches
her father's fire
burn, once again,
in the smithy fireplace,
thinks of Vulcan:

bluish flames
her father bellows
rise higher and higher
up the flue,
as glowing coals
split in two.

With luminous eyes,
the blacksmith's daughter,
years removed
from her father's fire,
now returns to
the beautiful girl
some Vulcan has
formed and shaped

and marvels at
the power and art
that can transform
metal, as a medium,
into a shape
that breathes.

Cuxland, the Coast

for Uta

They drive through evening fields,
dark clouds hanging in expansive sky.
Cows still graze in 10 p.m. pastures.
Wind hurtles in off the water, as they
walk up a dike and look out far
into the North Sea. Wind whips low
tide to a kind of confection. Great plain
of low water, dark-gray mud flats,
odor of muck, ships off in the distance.
A full moon tries to break through moody,
mysterious clouds. Her hair blowing wildly,
she smiles, says she loves wind. He says
he loves wind, rain, winter, clouds.
Listen to the wind, she says, do you hear it?
He hears the wheat whisper as North Sea wind
ripples and tousles it. She is of this place,
has brought him to see what she loves,
but explains nothing more than what
the wind, the sea, the mud, the moon reveal.
When they walk off the dike, the full moon breaks
through and darkness deepens over the North Sea.

The Lost Picture

She stands in a nineteenth-century
farmhouse, before a Dutch door
opened at the top. Behind her
blooms a garden of herbs.

He raises his camera,
clicks, after composing
this almost perfect scene.
But the film does not come
out of its roll properly,
and the image is lost.
You fill in the blanks.

What was the color
of her hair? Was it
brown tinged with red,
backlit by summer sun?
What was the color
of her eyes? Were they
pale blue, flashing with
light from a source
not part of the scene?

What was the cause
of her smile? Was this
the kind of house she
had always longed for,
a farmhouse in the country?
Did she feel strangely
at home in this place?

What herbs flourished
in the garden beyond
the door in front
of which she stood?
Lavender, rosemary,
sage, mother-of-thyme?

You fill in the blanks.
You complete the picture.
You tell the rest of the story.

IV.
GOD'S COUNTRY

God's Country

In God's country,
one hill always rolls
into another, trees that
grow taller toward dusk
set sail toward the horizon
when night moves in,
and the hoot owl cries
from deep in the dark,
on a sycamore branch
dangling across the creek.

When you steer around
a curve in God's country,
the language on the side
of the red barn coming
at you tells you what
tobacco to chew,
and a sign on the side
of the road tells you
when church begins.

In God's country,
a little boy who feels
Oscar Robertson's touch
shoots the eyes out
of the hoop his father bolted
to the side of the barn.

When your tires crunch
across the gravel
of a driveway
in God's country,
you coast, in your pickup,
to the last spot and park
next to the back porch.

Through the screen door,
your nose takes in the scent
that tells you onions have
lain down in bacon drippings
in the iron skillet and made
friends with potatoes boiled
in their jackets, sliced into
thin white coins of the realm,
and stacked up to the bottom
of the iron lid pressing down.

In God's country,
when you sit down at the table
to bless the stew that has
simmered on the stove,
your father's words surprise
you each time they flutter
out of his mouth, in the dialect
that his grandparents spoke
in that country the old ones,
once upon a time, left behind.

When you learn to speak
the old language in God's country,
you try to make an umlaut
by shaping a capital *o* with
your lips, but they relax.
What comes out is a long English
a as you give thanks: *Danke shane!*

In God's country,
the ancestors gather at night,
in the woods, to light a bonfire
that sends signals to you, on the hill,
so you will never feel lost
no matter how far you stray,

as long as you remember
where you came from
and never forget that to those
who came before you

where your family lives will
always remain God's country.

Polished Shoes

Every Saturday morning, I gathered
the six pairs of shoes we wore
(two adults, four children), lined them
up on my father's workbench,
in the furnace room of the basement,
brought them back to life again.

Some were black, some brown,
some oxblood, one pair was white.
I tried to treat them all with
the respect due a tried and proven
warrior, but I knew the liquid gook
I swabbed on them, to cover up
their scuffs and wounds, was
a quick fix that would scrape off
at the first touch. No manner
of parental praise for what
I had done could remove
the unclean feeling that lingered.

Only when I progressed to wax
polish did I take pride in my work.
I loved brushing the colored wax
into grains of leather and bringing
it to a luster with a green wool cloth
I rubbed back and forth until light
from the bulb above the workbench
bounced off the dozen smooth surfaces.

Decades later and a thousand
miles away from my Saturday chore,
a friend once asked why my shoes always
look new. Those six revived pairs
of shoes appeared, again, before
my eyes, reflecting light from the bulb
above my father's workbench
in that basement, and as I heard
that furnace kick on again, I gave
away my dark family secret:
Because I keep them polished.

A Pretty Small Town

There was once a pretty small town.
When I drove through it years ago,
in the summer, the clapboard houses
were sparkling white, people sat swinging
on front porches, and sparrows sang
in the canopy of sugar maples on both
sides of Main Street, which curved
at just the right angle. Nothing to change.

When I returned to find that street,
it no longer curved at the same place.
The houses that remained no longer
resembled the ones I once knew,
not a single swing swayed on a porch,
and neon fast-food joints puffed
smoke from burning patties of meat
in the midday sun, in clearings
where many maples once stood.

Before I could get my bearings,
I was funneled back onto the interstate.
Tires blabbed, horns blared, and semis
rolled past, but at my back, from time
to time, I still heard the creak of chains
holding up swings on long front porches.
Sometimes when I stared into the rear-
view mirror, I saw that Main Street
curve at just the right angle,
away from me, into the dark.

If you once lived in one
of those simple white houses,
please write me a letter, send me
a photograph of that curve that has
disappeared, tell me if you still
remember the song of sparrows
in those sugars maples
I sometimes think I imagined.

Second Sister

for Mary

Our mother waited for a daughter
who, unlike her first, would stay
on this earth for a time. We knew
we must not ask why she sometimes
cried. When the second sister came,
Mother started to hum again
as she dusted the furniture,
the pots on the stove steamed
hotter, and the wash dried cleaner
in the sun and smelled sweeter.
The corn grew taller in the garden,
and when the sun set on one side
of the house, it seemed to come up,
the next minute, on the other.
She was standing there
ready to raise the window higher
so the breeze could blow in from
the woods, and when the snow fell,
you could hear the cardinals
sing for more cracked corn and see
them settle on the branches
of the flowering almond she had
brought from her grandparents' house.
Then a toddler, second sister,
began to wobble around the green lawn
and bend down to touch the plants.

Prayers and Smoke

When light drained out
of the woods behind the house,
thunder clapped, and lighting
scarred the sky, Mother lit a candle
in front of the small shrine
to the Virgin, on the table
in the back hall. We knew
we must not speak.

When a storm was severe,
she pulled down the palm
stuck behind the framed print
of the Sacred Heart, touched
candle flame to dry tip,
and let smoke rise. We
held our breath as one.

When she could not
remember where she
had left or put something,
she prayed to St. Anthony,
said she knew she would
find it with his help, and did.
No way we could argue.

When our father's nerves
turned bad again, she
prayed to St. Jude, patron
of hopeless causes. When
they took him away for
shock treatment again,
we stood in puddles
of silence. Spirals
of fear rose like smoke.

Where the Waters Grow Deep

1

A small-town newspaper column
once told of the time a woman took her young
children swimming in the lake on the farm
of her brother, not far from town.

As this mother was sitting on a blanket,
gabbing with her sister-in-law, her younger son,
splashing in the shallow water, took off,
floating and kicking like a motorboat
escaped from its moorings, toward the middle
of the lake. He did not know how to swim.
Nor did his mother, who let out a yelp
and hit the water with her legs churning
like a fullback exploding into the line.

Her bare feet pushed off the sand
in the shallow water and then felt
an alarm when sand turned to mud,
as she entered a new zone of danger
and felt water deepen. Just at the last
split second, where the bottom was about
to fall out of the mud her toes could
still touch, she reached out and snagged
her wayward son by one last ankle
and pulled him back into her arms.

2

Yes, I was there. I do not remember
living through that incident, but I did
enter into the waters of that deepening
lake in my mother's retelling of the tale
to her brothers and sisters and in-laws,
whenever family got together. Which
was often. Now that I have a daughter
and son, who, in my mind, often veer
toward where the water grows deep,
and I know that although I swim well,
my stroke can never be good enough,
I shudder to think of what it felt like
to lunge forward at that critical point,
reach out with your last possible grasp,
to the point where your arm is about
to pull out of its joint, and try to hook
a son, headed unknowingly toward
the deep black waters, by the last
ankle you may ever see, as your
toes lose their grip in the mud.

Coming into Her Own

When our father's heart collapsed,
she wept but came into her own.
Now that he who had wrecked
his knee in a car crash when he
was young and could not tolerate
her learning how to drive was no
longer there to tremble beside her
and criticize because of his fear,

she started his car, in the garage,
backed it, downhill, out of his driveway,
and never stopped going
until she could no longer hold
the wheel steady or her feet
could not remember the difference
between the brake and the accelerator.

Now she would reduce the size
of her garden to fit her appetite
and the hunger of the children
and the grandchildren who came
back home, to sit at her table.
Now she would not have to beg
for money, worry about how long
it would last. Now she could sit
up as late as she liked, candlewicking
butterflies and bears on off-white
cushions she would give away
whenever a baby came into the world.
Now she could make as many quilts
as she wanted, to give to children,
grandchildren, nieces and nephews.

When the good years passed
and she knew there were few
days left to candlewick and quilt,
she saw it was time to finish what
she had started, so she could give
what she wanted to those she
would leave behind, and she did.

Aunt Verena

I found her in a reclining chair
in a lounge of the facility,
where others also looked like
appendages of the furniture.
There was little left to recognize.
She did not realize I was her nephew,
home for a visit, did not respond
to anything I said. As I held her hand,
my wife and children at my side,
I rubbed it and began to speak
in German. I said her name in the old
way, asked how she was doing, kept
asking questions in the language she
had heard as a little girl. Her eyes
rolled open a bit, closed, rolled open
again just a crack, and I could detect
a flicker of light, like what you see
in the woods when the dawn
breaks between clusters of leaves.
I wondered what scenes were replaying
in her mind, what voices she heard.
But then her eyelids fell back. There
was and would be no light, no sound.
I rubbed her hand once more, said
Auf Wiederseh'n, Tanti Verena,
knew it was time to turn and let go.

Elegy for Small-Town Heroes

Some of them sure could put
a bouncing ball through a hoop.

Some could pound the red stitches
off a horsehide cover with an ash stick.

Some could put a beautiful
spiral on an oval pigskin,

but when it came time to move on
beyond the applause at the end

of the game, they had nowhere
to go, and they began to suck

a bottle that made them breathe fire
and soup up cars that turned corners

and curves at breakneck speed.
They pumped gas at the station,

picked up their classmates' garbage,
turned fat faster than anybody else.

Some disappeared into factories
and never seemed ready to leave,

until they were laid out in a coffin.
Then all anybody could remember

to say was how good they had been
and what they could have become.

Where Trees Are Tall

Let me go where the trees
are tall and full and the breeze
lifts the leaves above your head
and the hound barks in the back
of the woods, to let you know
he smells your approach
riding on the wind and to warn
you that you shall never be able
to displace him from the territory
he has stamped with his scent
and knows deep down with his snoot,

for to move in the hills where
scent marks the measure
of what you are and how you
relate to all that lives
is to give yourself to the flow
of the wind and the patter of rain
and the contour of the land
and the lines of the trees
and the scud of the clouds
and the angle of sunlight
and the flight of the birds
and the cries of the mammals
and the song of what sings,
beyond our eyes and ears,
from what was here before
and carries us to what
lies above and beyond
where we have ever been.

Squirrel Hunter's Dream

Always there is a taller hickory tree
over the next hill, and cuttings are falling,
and fox squirrels are lifting their red
tails and exposing their bellies as they
crawl out to the ends of branches
that bend under their fleshy weight,
but you can never tiptoe close enough
without cracking a twig beneath your foot,
or you are too slow to lift your gun,
release the safety, and aim the barrel,
or one squirrel that was dropping shells
almost on the top of your head stops
eating and falls asleep, stretched out
flat on top of a wide branch, while
another starts cutting on the other side
of the tree, where your vision is blocked;
but this means you have found the best
shagbark hickory tree ever, since you have
never seen so many squirrels cutting on one tree
at the same time, and so when you roll over
and wake up you will still see all those
squirrels moving out to the ends of limbs,
to find another nut high above your head,
and cuttings will continue to fall,
and one day you will step just right
and find yourself in the perfect position,
at the right time, to raise your gun.

The Piankashaw in the Sycamore

Somewhere, I once read
that after the first Europeans
arrived in what has come to be
known as southern Indiana,
from Kentucky or Virginia,
an Indian was observed stretched
out on a big branch of a tree,
perhaps an ivory sycamore,
that hung out over the waters
of a bend in the Patoka River.

This was some time after
the Piankashaw had left
the area behind. Something
must have been terribly wrong,
the author implied, for this
man to return to the area
where he was born and make
himself so vulnerable.

What could have happened,
the author wanted to know,
to make the man risk his life
just to crawl up the trunk of that
ancient tree and stretch himself
out on a branch that dangled
over the waters of a river that
had flowed through the middle
of the life of his people for who
knows how many generations?

What could have happened
on or near that site to pull
the man back? Was it memory
of his people and their history
tied to that spot that made
him return and lie down
so high above the ground,
over the flowing sacred waters
and spirits he knew remained?

Had he come back to pay tribute
to the unmarked grave of a relative,
gather medicinal herbs, maybe
offer tobacco to Lennipeshewa,
man-panther who dwelt in the depths?

Was he given over to the power
of spirits connected with this tree
and the bend in the river
where he and his clan fished
when he was a boy?

Had he lost the desire to live
in some other place he knew
was separated from the spirits
of those who had come before?

Was he preparing to enter
the world where the spirits
of those who had once lived here
would welcome him back
from whence he had come?

Dark and Deep

When Robert Frost walked
in the woods, he had a sense
of where the trail would fork
but not where the branches
would lead or what darkness
or light or combination of the two
might lie beyond. It was
the thrill of not knowing where
he was going or what might come
that gave a slight bounce to his step,
as the dusk thickened and the dark
began to pull him on like a magnet,
at the back of a deep cave where
shadows flickered like a campfire.
He loved to stand in a hollow,
as if at the bottom of a well,
and look up at the snowflakes
falling heavily out of a starless
sky, landing on his eyelashes.
Part of him wanted to stay
there forever and just stare
as the woods filled with snow,
and part of him said you better
leave soon. The only way
he could find his way back
to where he had started from
was to compose in his mind,
in a language he had to discover,
a poem whose lines snaked
out of the dark and whose
rhythms moved his feet
to take the steps that led back
to where others liked to walk
and promises could be kept.

What I Found in the Woods

In the wild rolling woods where I hunted
squirrels by myself for the first time,
I heard a murmur of familiar voices,
in a language I only half understood,
rising from a hollow just over the hill.

When I finally reached the crest
and looked down between tall trees,
I saw a family huddled together
on the other side of the creek,
in peasant garb from the old country.

When they saw me standing there,
shotgun on shoulder, they uttered
cries of joy. "It's him!" they shouted
in unison, in words that the clear air
of early-morning woods translated
and transmitted into my ears.

"He has come to lead us home!"
said the mother with a clarity
beyond belief. "He looks like
one of us!" said the daughter in relief.
"He could be my big brother!"
said the son with a broad smile.
"Take us to the ones who came
after us," said the father,
with understated authority.

I raised my gun in the air,
fired a shot to celebrate
their arrival, just as I had seen
my father do on New Year's Eve,
but when the buckshot that
blasted the leaves settled
back down to the ground,
my family of missing ancestors
had disappeared and left me
standing alone in the woods.

Coming into the Valley

Finally I come into a valley
where tall white oaks and shagbark
hickories stand like giants whose
limbs I remember from another age.
Cuttings fall through layers of leaves,
as fox squirrels with creamy bellies
and bushy red tails bend the branches.

"Oh, I remember this place," I hear
myself say. My feet are happy they
have come to rest. Here I am home.

Now my vision enters a new stage
of clarity, objects come into focus,
my ears detect sounds from beyond,
and I see my father sitting on a log,
gazing up at the treetops. The lines
on his face are completely relaxed.
Puffs of smoke rise above the bowl
of his pipe. He sees me, waves,
whispers, "Glad you came!" "Me too,"
I say. "It took so long to get back
to this place. I thought I lost the way."

Then, in a stand of saplings beyond,
I hear a girl humming a familiar song.
When I walk over and part the leaves,
 I see my young mother stirring
corn mash fermenting in a kettle.
"Please don't tell anybody," she says
with a grin. "Nobody must know."
"Oh no, I won't," I assure her.

Further on, I hear the whir of a circular
saw that recently began to roll. Guiding
it into a felled length of white oak
is my grandfather Benno. His white
handlebar mustache is as thick
as leaves on the trees on every side.
As I approach, he turns off the saw,
motions for me to sit with him on the log.
"You've grown since I left," he says
with a simplicity as clear as the sunlight
flickering on the tips of his high-top shoes.

Over his shoulders stands his sister-in-law,
Great-Aunt Tillie, who spoke only German
when I visited her farm as a boy.
Now I understand every word she utters,
can express every nuance of affection
and affirmation in words in the tongue
that brings light into her blue eyes
the very same shade as my father's.

Now I have reached the point where
every word is a poem that all creatures
understand and love. I understand
everything they say in their language;
they understand everything I say in mine.
Not one of us needs to utter the poem
that the other already knows and lives.
There is no distinction between humans,
animals, and plants, between family and friends,
between friends and strangers, poetry and prose.

I share this moment with you, but I would
have you understand that not every step
that led to this recognition of union
in the leafy valley has been so blessed.
Behind the light that filters down from
the treetops, to where I now repose,
gathers a darkness that often pressed
on my shoulders and lay on my heart.

May you find the right steps to take
toward this spot, where I lie in wait.
Mention this poem and we shall talk.

Moon Shadows

for Elfrieda and Leon Fleck

I sit under a full moon,
at midnight, and see
shadows of trees on the far
side of the lake, lying
on the waters like spirits
from the other world
come back to visit.

Each time I look
away and back again,
the shadows extend
farther and closer
to the near shore.

When the shadows
cast by the moonlight
reach and absorb me,
I will know I have left
this world for the next.

May I return
to this land I love,
when the moon is full

and someone like you sits
in moonlight, with open eyes,
ready to receive

the shadows of trees
gliding over the waters,
toward the shore
where you live.

This Dust

. . . I only
borrowed this dust.
— Stanley Kunitz

This dust found
a pretty good world
to fall into,

but I find
nothing to celebrate
on my birthday.

I had nothing
to do with
my conception,

nothing to do
with being
pushed out
of the womb,

nothing to do
with the genes
I inherited
or the name
I was given.

Do not misunderstand.
I have no complaints.
I accept what
I have been given.

I would refuse
another name even
if it were easier
to spell or pronounce.

I crave nobody
else's genes

and would not
exchange this dust
for any other
or move onto
another planet.

128

I enjoy seeing
the sunlight play
on the leaves
of trees whose
names I love
to learn and say.

I enjoy many
of the people
who swirl into
my orbit

and most of
those who remain
in my constellation.

I care deeply
for the children
who call me
father

and the woman
who calls me
husband.

I speak gladly
in the voice
I have evolved
from those who
came before.

When this dust
I only borrowed
is given back
to the ground
it came from,

may the spirit
that animates it
find another world
equally good
and like spirits
to move around.

Legacy

My face will vanish
from the mirror.

The wind will not
blow in my hair;
sunlight will not
touch my forehead.

My ears will not
perceive the patter
of rain on leaves.

My fingertips will not
smell of the rosemary
I love to stroke;

my tongue will no longer
savor the flavors
of cinnamon and words.

My voice will withdraw
from the air but remain
alive in the poems
printed on the page.

Say those words out
loud and you shall see
me in the mirror,
standing behind you,

and feel the pulse
of my breath
on your lips.

Blood Song

for Wolfgang Buck

When I take leave
of this physical world,
may my spirit find
its way back as song
that flows in your blood.

Let the bass lay
a solid foundation,
the drum kick
my lyric along,
and the lead guitar
drive the melody

that carries my vision
all the way back
to your heart,
so you may pump it
and pass it along
to those who follow.

Genug um zu geniessen / Enough to Enjoy

for Petra and Helmut Haberkamm

I sat on a bench in a barn
in the region of my ancestors
and listened to a songwriter sing
songs about his life, in Franconian
dialect, and my friend read poems
in the same tongue I heard the oldest
relatives speak when I was a boy
in southern Indiana. When a reporter
asked me how much I could understand,
I found myself saying words
that came together in my mouth
for the first time:
Genug um zu geniessen.

The next day, when I read to
Franconian high-school students
my poems in English about
growing up in southern Indiana
and coming to places where
my family had lived in their country,
I advised them not to worry about
grasping every word. I told the story
of what the reporter had asked
that night in the barn and passed
along the phrase I found in their
language, to express what they might
settle for as they sat back to listen:
Genug um zu geniessen.

The next day, when I took a walk
along a lane that wound through
fields of barley, rye, and wheat,
I thought of the suffering my
mother endured when she battled
cancer, the problems my daughter
was having with a boyfriend,
and the depression that came over
me and my wife when our son
*

had to be hospitalized for an illness
he could not recognize. At my feet
I saw pink and blue wildflowers
I picked for the German friends
who opened their door and gave
me a bed in a bad time. I could
not give names to the flowers
I brought them, but when I asked
myself how I felt about the life
I had been given and how much
of it I could understand, I said,
Genug um zu geniessen.

When I ask myself if it is unfair
that my time on this earth is limited,
those I love have problems I cannot
solve, and the language I speak
does not always express the nuances
of what I feel or the ideas others
try to communicate to me, I recall
the question the reporter put to me
that night in the barn in Franconia,
and I repeat to myself that what has
been given to me as a life to live is
genug um zu geniessen.

The Time Has Come

The time has come
to come home, Mother.
I've followed the river
all the way to the sea,
stood where tall buildings
poked into the clouds,
and it's time to come
home to where the tulip
poplar stands prouder
than anything man can
build up from the ground.

The time has come
to come home, Mother.
I want to hear
the hickory nut fall
through crisp leaves
and splatter onto the ground.
I want to hear
the turtledove coo
in the pines, at dusk.

The time has come
to come home, Mother.
I feel pain rising
in my bones, and I
want to stand and give
thanks where you lie
in the good earth
and watch the sun
set on the hills
where it rose
when I was a boy.

The time has come
to come home, Mother.
I can hear your quiet
voice sing those words,
and the tune is right.

EPILOGUE

The Audience of the Dead

I have come to understand
I must write for the dead.

The living must be excused.
They have other concerns.

Unlike the living, the dead
must have their poems, or they
lose touch with those they love.

Because the dead have grown
into the fullness of their being,
they cannot be fooled.

Because they know everyone will one
day have what they have already earned,
they play no favorites, make no promises.

Yet they are approachable.
Mere cleverness leaves them cold.
Technical virtuosity won't touch them.
Honesty alone will not reach them.

What they demand is that we
discover all they now know
about what they left behind.

Because every day there are more
of them but there is just one of me,
each poem becomes harder to write.

But who could resist the challenge
of reaching the ultimate audience?

I might even be trying to reach you.
I might even be trying to reach myself.

BIOGRAPHICAL NOTES

NORBERT KRAPF grew up in Jasper, Indiana, a German community, and taught, from 1970 to 2004, at Long Island University, where he directed the C. W. Post Poetry Center for eighteen years. He now lives in Indianapolis. A graduate of St. Joseph's College (Rensselaer, Indiana), which awarded him an honorary doctorate, he received his M.A. and Ph.D. in English and American Literature from the University of Notre Dame. His poetry volumes include the trilogy *Somewhere in Southern Indiana*, *Blue-Eyed Grass: Poems of Germany*, and *Bittersweet Along the Expressway: Poems of Long Island*, as well as the recent *The Country I Come From*, nominated for the Pulitzer Prize. He is the editor of *Finding the Grain*, a collection of pioneer German journals and letters from his native Dubois County, and *Under Open Sky*, a gathering of writings, by contemporary American poets, on William Cullen Bryant. He is also the translator/editor of *Shadows on the Sundial: Selected Early Poems of Rainer Maria Rilke* and *Beneath the Cherry Sapling: Legends from Franconia*. Winner of the Lucille Medwick Memorial Award from the Poetry Society of America, he has been a U.S. Exchange Teacher at West Oxon Technical College, England, and Fulbright Professor of American Poetry at the Universities of Freiburg and Erlangen-Nuremberg, Germany. For more information, see **www.krapfpoetry.com**.

German photographer ANDREAS RIEDEL was born in 1970, in Neustadt an der Aisch, in Norbert Krapf's ancestral region of Franconia. Riedel was an apprentice in a photography studio from 1987 to 1990. In 1994, he passed his examination as a master photographer and since 1993 has worked as a freelance photographer in his own studio. In 1997, he received two Kodak European Portrait Gold Awards. The black-and-white photos that inspired Norbert Krapf's sequence in this collection, "Franconian Faces and Fields," were originally published in Riedel's *Die sedd'n un' die selln* (1997). He collaborated with Franconian dialect poet Helmut Haberkamm in *Lichd ab vom Schuss* and *Des sichd eich gleich*. For additional samples of Andreas Riedel's work and further information, see **www.fotografie-riedel.de**.

OTHER POETRY AND SHORT FICTIONS AVAILABLE FROM TIME BEING BOOKS

YAKOV AZRIEL

Threads from a Coat of Many Colors: Poems on Genesis

EDWARD BOCCIA

No Matter How Good the Light Is: Poems by a Painter

LOUIS DANIEL BRODSKY

You Can't Go Back, Exactly
The Thorough Earth
Four and Twenty Blackbirds Soaring
Mississippi Vistas: Volume One of *A Mississippi Trilogy*
Falling from Heaven: Holocaust Poems of a Jew and a Gentile *(Brodsky and Heyen)*
Forever, for Now: Poems for a Later Love
Mistress Mississippi: Volume Three of *A Mississippi Trilogy*
A Gleam in the Eye: Poems for a First Baby
Gestapo Crows: Holocaust Poems
The Capital Café: Poems of Redneck, U.S.A.
Disappearing in Mississippi Latitudes: Volume Two of *A Mississippi Trilogy*
Paper-Whites for Lady Jane: Poems of a Midlife Love Affair
The Complete Poems of Louis Daniel Brodsky: Volume One, 1963–1967
Three Early Books of Poems by Louis Daniel Brodsky, 1967–1969: *The Easy Philosopher, "A Hard Coming of It" and Other Poems*, and *The Foul Rag-and-Bone Shop*
The Eleventh Lost Tribe: Poems of the Holocaust
Toward the Torah, Soaring: Poems of the Renascence of Faith
Yellow Bricks *(short fictions)*
Catchin' the Drift o' the Draft *(short fictions)*
This Here's a Merica *(short fictions)*
Voice Within the Void: Poems of *Homo supinus*
Leaky Tubs *(short fictions)*
Shadow War: A Poetic Chronicle of September 11 and Beyond, Volume One
The Complete Poems of Louis Daniel Brodsky: Volume Two, 1967–1976
Shadow War: A Poetic Chronicle of September 11 and Beyond, Volume Two
Shadow War: A Poetic Chronicle of September 11 and Beyond, Volume Three
Shadow War: A Poetic Chronicle of September 11 and Beyond, Volume Four
Shadow War: A Poetic Chronicle of September 11 and Beyond, Volume Five
Rated Xmas *(short fictions)*
Nuts to You! *(short fictions)*
The Complete Poems of Louis Daniel Brodsky: Volume Three, 1976–1980

HARRY JAMES CARGAS *(EDITOR)*

Telling the Tale: A Tribute to Elie Wiesel on the Occasion of His 65th Birthday — Essays, Reflections, and Poems

(866) 840-4334
HTTP://WWW.TIMEBEING.COM

JUDITH CHALMER

Out of History's Junk Jar: Poems of a Mixed Inheritance

GERALD EARLY

How the War in the Streets Is Won: Poems on the Quest of Love and Faith

GARY FINCKE

Blood Ties: Working-Class Poems

ALBERT GOLDBARTH

A Lineage of Ragpickers, Songpluckers, Elegiasts & Jewelers: Selected Poems
of Jewish Family Life, 1973–1995

ROBERT HAMBLIN

From the Ground Up: Poems of One Southerner's Passage to Adulthood

WILLIAM HEYEN

Erika: Poems of the Holocaust
Falling from Heaven: Holocaust Poems of a Jew and a Gentile *(Brodsky and Heyen)*
Pterodactyl Rose: Poems of Ecology
Ribbons: The Gulf War — A Poem
The Host: Selected Poems, 1965–1990

TED HIRSCHFIELD

German Requiem: Poems of the War and the Atonement of a Third Reich Child

VIRGINIA V. JAMES HLAVSA

Waking October Leaves: Reanimations by a Small-Town Girl

RODGER KAMENETZ

The Missing Jew: New and Selected Poems
Stuck: Poems Midlife

NORBERT KRAPF

Somewhere in Southern Indiana: Poems of Midwestern Origins
Blue-Eyed Grass: Poems of Germany

(866) 840-4334
HTTP://WWW.TIMEBEING.COM

ADRIAN C. LOUIS

Blood Thirsty Savages

LEO LUKE MARCELLO

Nothing Grows in One Place Forever: Poems of a Sicilian American

GARDNER MCFALL

The Pilot's Daughter

JOSEPH MEREDITH

Hunter's Moon: Poems from Boyhood to Manhood

BEN MILDER

The Good Book Says . . . : Light Verse to Illuminate the Old Testament
The Good Book Also Says . . . : Numerous Humorous Poems Inspired by the
    New Testament
Love Is Funny, Love Is Sad
The Zoo You Never Gnu: A Mad Menagerie of Bizarre Beasts and Birds

CHARLES MUÑOZ

Fragments of a Myth: Modern Poems on Ancient Themes

MICHEAL O'SIADHAIL

The Gossamer Wall: Poems in Witness to the Holocaust

JOSEPH STANTON

Imaginary Museum: Poems on Art